MONDAY
NIGHT
MOCKTAILS

MONDAY

52 Drinks

NIGHT

to Welcome the Week

MOCKTAILS

BY JENNIFER NEWENS

THE
collective.
BOOK STUDIO

Library of Congress Cataloging-in-Publication
Data available.
ISBN: 978-1-68555-769-0
Ebook ISBN: 978-1-68555-931-1
Library of Congress Control Number: 202493118

Printed using Forest Stewardship Council
certified stock from sustainably
managed forests.

Manufactured in China.

Design by Rachel Lopez Metzger.

Photo credits:
Licensed from Shutterstock.com: all pages,
except for 12, 34, 42, 44, 47, 67, 80, 106, 130, 138

10 9 8 7 6 5 4 3 2 1

The Collective Book Studio®
Oakland, California
www.thecollectivebook.studio

To Paul, my taster for life,
and Sal & Stella, my furry
kitchen helpers.

CONTENTS

a tiny bit about mocktails . . .

There are many reasons to drink a zero-proof cocktail, also known as a mocktail, whether it's for health reasons or that you're simply trying to add a little flair to your nightly beverage routine. This book will help you do just that: Organized seasonally, there is a special drink for every Monday of the year. Though most recipes are scaled for one or two, there are a handful that serve a crowd—perfect for an office party, a get-together with colleagues, or a three-day weekend barbecue. And, of course, who's to say you need to reserve the drinks for only Mondays?

Many of the drinks are inspired by classic cocktails, mixed with one or more of the growing numbers of high-quality nonalcoholic (NA) wine or beer options and zero-proof distilled spirits available today. Other mocktails have been developed to enhance some of the wonderful nonalcoholic products in today's marketplace, like shrubs, kombuchas, and hop waters, or to show off fresh fruit during its peak season. Note that nonalcoholic spirits do not taste the same sipped straight as their alcoholic counterparts, but mixed with other ingredients in a mocktail, they can be fine approximations to their boozy cousins.

I'm lucky that there is a retail store near where I live devoted to nonalcoholic wines and spirits. I'm able to walk in, discuss with the salesclerk what I'm looking for, and walk out the door with a recommendation for exactly what I need. If a store like this is not available to you, I provide a list of resources on page 146 where you can source ingredients online.

I consider a mocktail every bit as special as its boozy counterpart, so I've borrowed the mixology methods from professional bartenders. For each of these recipes, I suggest a glass type, mixing method, and garnish to make the most of the ingredients and make every drink special—even on a Monday. ENJOY!

a tiny bit about barware ...

Cocktail shaker

There are two common types of shakers: cobbler and Boston. A cobbler shaker includes a cup basin with a detachable top, measuring cap, and strainer. A Boston shaker uses two weighted metal cups that seal together to quickly mix multiple drinks.

Mixing glass

As the older brother to the cocktail shaker, the mixing glass serves a similar purpose, though it generally produces a less-diluted cocktail. A mixing glass requires the use of a strainer and a bar spoon.

Strainer

The most common strainer is the Hawthorne strainer, which is all you'll need for most cocktails. If you want a finer strain, such as when you are using seedy berries, you can use a fine-mesh sieve.

Bar spoon

While any spoon will technically work for mixing a cocktail, the traditional bar spoon has an extra-long handle to keep the bartender's fingers away from the drink and give extra mobility when stirring.

Jigger or measured shot glass

A jigger is a liquid measuring tool designed specifically for cocktail mixing. It notes common measurements and comes in several sizes.

Citrus press

The mocktails in this book recommend the use of fresh citrus juice whenever possible. A handheld citrus press is an easy-to-use and nearly irreplaceable tool when extracting fresh lime or lemon juice at home. A larger citrus juicer is helpful for orange and grapefruit juice.

Muddler

A muddler is a simple wooden or metal tool resembling a miniature baseball bat with a long handle and a flat bottom. It works to mash ingredients to express their flavors and aromas before adding the liquids for mocktails and cocktails.

a tiny bit about glassware ...

Cocktail glasses come in all shapes and sizes. While each recipe notes the traditional glassware used, the real star of the show will always be the drink itself. Below is a list of the glassware in this book, but you can pour your Monday night mocktail into any vessel you choose.

Brandy snifter or balloon glass	Old fashioned or lowball glass	Highball or Collins glass
Martini	Margarita	Mug
Coupe	Pint glass	Wineglass
Champagne flute	Julep cup	Copper mule mug
	Daiquiri	

SPRING

MARCH

MAY

VIRGIN MARGARITA

I developed this recipe to be simple, using just three liquid ingredients. It's easy to customize to your own tastes. For example, my husband likes it on the sweeter side, so I add more agave to his. I like mine tarter, so I add more lime juice. When I'm not in the mood to make the fancy salt-sugar rim, I simply add a pinch of salt to the cocktail shaker, which makes all the flavors pop.

GLASS: Margarita	GARNISH: Lime slice
2 tsp salt, for the rim	½ oz/15 ml fresh lime juice
1 tsp sugar, for the rim	⅓ oz/10 ml agave nectar or maple syrup
Lime wedge, for the rim	Lime slice, for garnish
2 oz/60 ml high-quality zero-proof tequila	

To prepare the glass, sprinkle the salt and sugar onto a small plate. Wipe the lime wedge around the edge of a cocktail glass, then dip the rim into the salt and sugar mixture.

In a cocktail shaker, add the tequila, lime juice, and agave. Add ice and shake until chilled. Strain into a cocktail glass with crushed ice and garnish with a lime slice. Makes 1 mocktail.

SPANISH-STYLE GIN AND TONIC

I was surprised to learn recently that Spain is as famous for gin and tonics as England is. In Spain, the simple cocktail is bolstered with herbs, spices, and other colorful and aromatic ingredients to make it as pleasing to the eye as it is to the palate. Be sure to use the best ingredients you can find for this drink, as they really matter here.

GLASS: Brandy snifter or balloon	GARNISH: Cucumber or citrus slices
4 oz/120 ml chilled high-quality tonic water	Small fresh herb sprigs: mint, thyme, basil, for garnish
2 oz/60 ml chilled high-quality zero-proof gin	Edible flowers, for garnish
Cucumber or citrus slices of your choice, for garnish	Spices: peppercorns, juniper berries, star anise, for garnish

Fill a cocktail glass with ice. Add the tonic water and gin. Garnish with the fresh citrus slices, herb sprigs, edible flowers, and spices of choice. Makes 1 mocktail.

BERRY DAIQUIRINI

A traditional daiquiri, a combination of rum, sugar, and lime juice, was my inspiration for this mocktail, with the addition of seasonal spring berries muddled into the mix. While you're sipping it, know that the berries also provide vitamin C and heart-healthy compounds. You may want to strain this using a fine-mesh sieve, as the berries contain a lot of seeds.

GLASS: Coupe	GARNISH: Raspberry or blackberry
2 strawberries	1 oz/30 ml fresh lime juice
2 raspberries, plus 1 for garnish	1 oz/30 ml Simple Syrup (see Tip, page 20)
1 blackberry, plus 1 for garnish	Fresh raspberry or blackberry, for garnish
2 oz/60 ml high-quality zero-proof rum	

In a cocktail shaker, muddle the strawberries, 2 raspberries, and 1 blackberry. Add the rum, lime juice, and simple syrup. Add ice and shake until chilled. Strain into a cocktail glass and garnish with a raspberry and a blackberry. Makes 1 mocktail.

Simple Syrup

Combine 1 cup/200 g granulated sugar
with 8 oz/240 ml water in a small saucepan.
Bring to a boil and simmer until the sugar is
dissolved, about 10 minutes. Cool completely,
then store in an airtight container.
Makes 12 oz/360 ml.

Brown Sugar Simple Syrup
Substitute dark brown sugar
for the granulated sugar.

Juniper Simple Syrup
After boiling, add 1 Tbsp juniper berries,
crushed, and 2 strips lemon zest.
Let stand for at least 2 hours, preferably
overnight. Strain before using.

Rosemary or Thyme Simple Syrup
After boiling, add 1–2 sprigs fresh rosemary or thyme. Let stand for at least 2 hours, preferably overnight.

Star Anise Simple Syrup
After boiling, add 4 whole star anise. Let stand for at least 2 hours, preferably overnight.

Turmeric Simple Syrup
After boiling, add 1 Tbsp turmeric powder. Let stand for at least 2 hours, preferably overnight, before using.

Vanilla Simple Syrup
After boiling, add 1 vanilla bean, split lengthwise. Let stand for several hours, preferably overnight.

GRAPEFRUIT FIZZ

With the rise in popularity of nonalcoholic beverages, new products are appearing in the marketplace to satisfy the thirst for alternatives to boozy drinks. Hop water, a fizzy blend of sparkling water and aromatic hops, is one of my favorite new items. It pairs beautifully with grapefruit juice, thyme simple syrup, and a touch of lime juice in this pretty drink.

GLASS: Old fashioned or lowball	GARNISH: Fresh thyme sprigs and grapefruit slices

2 oz/60 ml fresh pink grapefruit juice

1 oz/30 ml fresh lime juice

1 oz/30 ml Thyme Simple Syrup (see Tip, page 21)

Chilled hop water

Fresh thyme sprigs and grapefruit slices, for garnish

Add the grapefruit juice, lime juice, and simple syrup to a cocktail glass and stir until mixed. Add ice. Top the glass with hop water and stir gently. Garnish with thyme sprigs and grapefruit slices. Makes 1 mocktail.

ELDERFLOWER SPRITZ

Here, elderflower syrup and nonalcoholic sparkling wine combine in a sophisticated sip for a warm spring evening. You'll want to choose a sparkling wine that you like to sip on its own; experiment to find your favorites. The elderflower syrup is also great mixed with sparkling water and can be used as a delicate syrup for pancakes or waffles.

GLASS: Old fashioned or lowball	GARNISH: Edible flowers or lemon slice

3 oz/90 ml high-quality nonalcoholic sparkling white wine

1 oz/30 ml sparkling water

1 oz/30 ml elderflower syrup

½ oz/15 ml fresh lemon juice

Edible flowers or lemon twist, for garnish

Fill a cocktail glass halfway with ice. Add the sparkling wine, sparkling water, elderflower syrup, and lemon juice. Stir to combine. Garnish with flowers or a lemon twist. Makes 1 mocktail.

SPICED MANGO MOCKTAIL

Simple syrups are your secret weapon when making mocktails. First, their viscosity mimics that of alcohol, helping create a satisfying mouthfeel. Second, they're super easy to flavor, giving you dozens of ways to spice up your drinks. Here, warm, sweet, licorice-like star anise lends its fragrance to a tropical mango concoction. When making the fruit puree, use water instead of simple syrup.

GLASS: Lowball	GARNISH: Whole star anise

2 oz/60 ml mango puree

2 oz/60 ml high-quality zero-proof rum

½–¾ oz/15–22 ml Star Anise Simple Syrup (see Tip, page 21), depending on the sweetness of the mango

½ oz/15 ml fresh lime juice

Whole star anise, for garnish

In a cocktail shaker, add the mango puree, rum, simple syrup, and lime juice. Add ice and shake until chilled. Strain into a cocktail glass and garnish with a star anise. Makes 1 mocktail.

FAUXJITO

This refreshing drink doesn't need any spirits—the combination of the brown sugar syrup and lime juice tastes just like it was made with rum. The simple formula is easy to experiment with, too: Try basil or different mint varieties; use lemon juice in place of the lime; choose honey or maple syrup instead of the simple syrup; or try different flavors of sparkling water.

GLASS: Highball	GARNISH: Mint sprig and lime wedges

10 fresh mint leaves

2 oz/60 ml fresh lime juice

1½ oz/45 ml Brown Sugar Simple Syrup (see Tip, page 20)

Sparkling water

Fresh mint sprig and lime wedges, for garnish

In a cocktail glass, muddle the mint leaves. Add the lime juice and simple syrup and stir. Fill the glass with ice, then top with sparkling water. Garnish with a mint sprig. Makes 1 mocktail.

How to Muddle

Muddling is used to gently "bruise" ingredients like herbs, as in a Mojito, or fruit, as in an Old Fashioned, to release their flavors and aromas. To muddle, place the called-for ingredients in the bottom of a cocktail shaker or sturdy glass. Insert the muddler, then press and twist the ingredients to express their flavors. Unless otherwise called for, a light touch is usually all that's needed.

NEW FASHIONED

|

This recipe is based on an old-timey American way to create an Old Fashioned cocktail that muddles sweet fruit with bourbon and sugar. I make it "new" by using Italian Amarena cherries instead of maraschino cherries and subbing in nonalcoholic bourbon. You'll feel sophisticated drinking it but won't wake up with a headache.

GLASS: Old fashioned or lowball	GARNISH: Orange twist

1 demerara sugar cube

4 dashes nonalcoholic bitters

2 Amarena cherries in syrup

1 orange slice, peeled

3 oz/90 ml high-quality zero-proof bourbon

Orange twist, for garnish

Put the sugar cube in a cocktail shaker and coat it with the bitters. Add the cherries and orange slice and muddle the mixture together vigorously. Add the bourbon and ice and shake until chilled. Strain into a cocktail glass with ice and garnish with an orange twist. Makes 1 mocktail.

BASIL JULEP

|

This drink is a riff on a mint julep, the traditional drink served at the Kentucky Derby, which is held on the first Saturday in May each year. Instead of fresh mint, I use fresh basil, but you can opt for the original herb if it suits you. I stick to the time-honored convention of serving the drink over crushed ice in a metal julep cup, where the drink gets nice and frosty. But, any festive glass will do.

GLASS: Julep cup or highball	GARNISH: Basil leaf and lime wedge
8 fresh basil leaves, plus 1 for garnish 2 oz/60 ml high-quality zero-proof bourbon	1½ oz/45 ml fresh lime juice 1 oz/30 ml Simple Syrup (see Tip, page 20) Lime wedge, for garnish

In a cocktail shaker, muddle 8 of the basil leaves. Add the bourbon, lime juice, and simple syrup. Add ice and shake until chilled. Strain into a julep cup filled with crushed ice and garnish with a lime wedge and the remaining basil leaf. Makes 1 mocktail.

BLACKBERRY SPARKLER

The blend of lemon juice and juniper syrup evokes the essence of gin in this mocktail. Because blackberries have lots of seeds, use a fine-mesh strainer to remove them in lieu of a regular cocktail strainer. Thanks to the berries, the drink is a lovely deep purple color.

GLASS: Old fashioned or lowball		GARNISH: Blackberries and mint sprig

4 fresh blackberries, plus 3 for garnish

½ oz/15 ml Juniper Simple Syrup (see Tip, page 20)

Lemon wedge

5 oz/150 ml high-quality nonalcoholic sparkling white wine

Fresh mint sprig, for garnish

In a mixing glass, muddle 4 of the blackberries. Add the simple syrup and a squeeze of lemon juice. Add the sparkling wine and stir. Strain into a cocktail glass filled with ice. Garnish with the remaining 3 blackberries and a mint sprig. Makes 1 mocktail.

STRAWBERRY SHRUB MOCKTAIL

Also called drinking vinegars, shrubs are vinegar- and sugar-based syrups blended with sugar, spices, and aromatics. They have existed for centuries but have recently exploded in popularity. Bartenders use them for cocktails and booze-free concoctions alike. Try shrubs on their own mixed with sparkling water to taste. Or mix them with zero-proof liquors, as I've done here.

GLASS: Lowball	GARNISH: Strawberry

1½ oz/45 ml high-quality zero-proof tequila

1 oz/30 ml strawberry shrub

Dash of nonalcoholic bitters (optional)

4 oz/120 ml sparkling water

Fresh strawberry, for garnish (optional)

In a cocktail glass, add the tequila, shrub, bitters (if using), and sparkling water. Add ice and stir until chilled. Garnish with a strawberry. Makes 1 mocktail.

MEYER LEMON COLLINS

Meyer lemons are native to Northern California, where I live. The flavor is like a cross between a lemon and a Mandarin orange, with a perfumed fragrance. They're becoming more and more available elsewhere, especially between December and May, when they're in season. If you can't find them, ask a friend in California to send some to you—they will change your life! Or you can use regular lemons for this recipe—you may want to add more honey and a splash of tangerine juice.

GLASS: Highball or Collins		GARNISH: Cocktail cherry and lemon slice
2 oz/60 ml high-quality zero-proof gin 1 oz/30 ml fresh Meyer lemon juice ¾ oz/22 ml local honey		Sparkling water Cocktail cherry, for garnish Lemon slice, for garnish

In a cocktail shaker, add the gin, lemon juice, and honey. Add ice and shake until chilled. Strain into a cocktail glass with ice and top with sparkling water. Garnish with a cherry and lemon slice. Makes 1 mocktail.

CHERRY MASH

This is a special mocktail to wait for when cherry season arrives. In smash-style drinks, you don't want to strain the cocktail after shaking. It's all about the fruit! You can also use sour cherries for this, just up the sugar and decrease the lemon juice a bit.

GLASS: Old fashioned or highball	GARNISH: Lemon slice and fresh cherry

8 fresh cherries, pitted, plus 1 cherry for garnish

2 Tbsp brown sugar

3 oz/90 ml high-quality zero-proof bourbon or rum

½ oz/15 ml fresh lemon juice

Lemon slice, for garnish

In a cocktail glass, muddle the cherries with the brown sugar. Add the bourbon and lemon juice and stir gently. Add ice and garnish with a lemon slice and a fresh cherry. Makes 1 mocktail.

SUMMER

KOMBUCHA COOLER

One of my favorite flavor combinations is strawberries and fresh basil, which are both in season in early summer. Here they pair in a refreshing drink with a kombucha base. When buying kombucha, be careful that the alcohol content is below 0.5% (the federal designation for a "nonalcoholic" beverage). Some brands contain higher ABV levels.

GLASS: Highball or collins	GARNISH: Lemon wedge

4 large strawberries

3 large basil leaves

12 oz/360 ml berry kombucha

½ oz/15 ml fresh lemon juice

Lemon wedge, for garnish

In a mixing glass, muddle the strawberries and basil leaf. Add the kombucha and lemon juice, stir, and strain into a cocktail glass filled with ice. Garnish with a lemon wedge. Makes 1 mocktail.

PINEAPPLE BEBIDA

Peak pineapple season runs March through July, so summer is a perfect time to make this bubbly Mexican-style drink that'll remind you of the beach.

GLASS: Old fashioned or lowball	GARNISH: Pineapple slice and jalapeño slices

Chile Salt, for the rim (see Tip, page 89)	½ oz/15 ml fresh lime juice
Lime wedge, for the rim	½ oz/15 ml agave nectar
1½ oz/45 ml Pineapple Shrub (see Tip, page 51)	Sparkling water
1½ oz/45 ml high-quality zero-proof tequila	Pineapple and jalapeño slices, for garnish

To prepare the glass, sprinkle the chile salt mixture onto a small plate. Wipe the lime wedge around the edge of the cocktail glass and reserve it for garnish. Dip the rim of the glass in the chile salt mixture. Fill the glass with ice.

In a cocktail shaker, add the shrub, tequila, lime juice, and agave. Add ice and shake until chilled. Strain into the prepared cocktail glass and top with sparkling water.

Garnish with pineapple and jalapeño slices. Makes 1 mocktail.

Pineapple Shrub

Peel, core, and chop a ripe pineapple. Measure 2 cups/240 g pineapple chunks and place them in a saucepan with 1 cup/240 ml water. Place over high heat. As soon as it comes to a boil, decrease the heat to low and simmer for 15 minutes. Stir in 1 cup/200 grams brown sugar until dissolved. Strain through a fine-mesh sieve and stir in 4–8 oz/120–240 ml apple cider vinegar. Let cool completely and chill.

FROZAY

When the weather starts to warm up, a rosé slushie makes a great end to the day. You can freeze the cubes ahead of time and keep them in the freezer.

GLASS: Coupe	GARNISH: Citrus slices and edible flowers
10 fresh strawberries (fewer if large) 1 bottle (750 ml) high-quality nonalcoholic rosé 8 oz/240 ml Simple Syrup (see Tip, page 20)	3 oz/90 ml fresh lemon juice 4 oz/120 ml high-quality zero-proof vodka Citrus slices and edible flowers, for garnish

Suspend a sieve over a bowl. Using a muddler, mash the strawberries through the sieve. Discard the solids. Add the rosé, simple syrup, and lemon juice to the bowl and stir well. Ladle the mixture into cube trays and freeze until solid.

When ready to serve, start a blender and toss in the frozen cubes through the hole in the blender lid. Stop the blender and add the vodka. Blend until slushy. Divide among cocktail glasses and garnish with citrus slices and edible flowers. Makes 4–5 mocktails.

VIRGIN MARIA

Here is a Mexican-style take on a Bloody Mary, featuring zero-proof tequila instead of vodka, and fresh cilantro and pickled jalapeño juice. Look for fresh tomato juice at your farmers' markets or run sun-ripened tomatoes through a juice extractor at home for best results. Alternatively, you can mail-order canned tomato juice from Happy Girl Kitchen (see Resources, page 146).

GLASS: Lowball	GARNISH: Jalapeños, lime wedge, and cilantro
6 oz/180 ml chilled high-quality tomato juice	½ oz/15 ml fresh lime juice
2 oz/60 ml high-quality zero-proof tequila	½ tsp celery salt
2 Tbsp chopped fresh cilantro	Cayenne pepper, to taste
½ oz/15 ml pickled jalapeño juice	Jalapeño slices, lime wedge, and cilantro sprigs, for garnish

Pour the tomato juice and tequila into a cocktail glass. Add the cilantro, jalapeño juice, lime juice, and celery salt and stir well. If you like some heat, stir in a bit of cayenne to taste. Garnish with jalapeño slices, lime wedges, and cilantro sprigs. Makes 1 mocktail.

WATERMELON-GINGER COOLER

Years ago, I worked on a book with the founder of Urban Remedy, an organic food and juice brand located in the San Francisco Bay Area. In the summer, they offer a cold-pressed watermelon-ginger juice that I adore. That delicious and refreshing combination of cooling watermelon and spicy ginger inspired this mocktail.

GLASS: Coupe	GARNISH: Watermelon slice and mint sprig
1 cup/140 g cubed watermelon	1 oz/30 ml agave nectar
2 tsp peeled chopped fresh ginger	1 cup/150 g ice cubes
1 oz/30 ml fresh lime juice	Sparkling water
	Watermelon slice and fresh mint sprig, for garnish

Put the watermelon, ginger, lime juice, agave, and ice in a blender and blend until smooth. Pour into a cocktail glass filled with ice. Top off with sparkling water and stir gently. Garnish with a watermelon slice and mint sprig. Makes 1 mocktail.

ITALIAN-STYLE SPRITZ

On our honeymoon in Italy, we drank spritzes everywhere we went: Rome, Florence, Sienna, Venice. It seemed like everyone was drinking them in the piazzas. This recipe is inspired by that trip, featuring the pleasantly bitter taste of an "Italian-style aperitif" (there are many nonalcoholic versions available now) with a mixture of NA sparkling wine and sparkling water.

GLASS: Wineglass	GARNISH: Orange wheel

2 oz/60 ml high-quality nonalcoholic aperitif

2 oz/60 ml high-quality nonalcoholic sparkling wine

2 oz/60 ml sparkling water

½ oz/15 ml high-quality zero-proof orange liqueur (optional)

Dash of nonalcoholic bitters (optional)

1 orange wheel, for garnish

Fill a cocktail glass with ice. Add the aperitif, sparkling wine, sparkling water, orange liqueur if you like it a bit sweeter, and bitters (if using). Stir gently. Garnish with an orange wheel. Makes 1 mocktail.

THAI PIÑA COLADA

*There are so many recipes for piña coladas,
so I wanted to add a little twist for mine.
For best results, use a high-speed blender
here, which will pulverize the lime leaves and
ice cubes into a smooth and frothy texture.*

GLASS: Wineglass	GARNISH: Pineapple slice
1 cup/200 g fresh pineapple chunks	2 oz/60 ml Brown Sugar Simple Syrup (see Tip, page 20)
1 cup/150 g ice cubes	1–2 fresh makrut lime leaves
Cream from 1 can (13.5 oz/ 380 ml) full-fat coconut milk	1 oz/30 ml fresh lime juice
4 oz/120 ml high-quality zero-proof rum	2 pineapple slices, for garnish

Put the pineapple chunks, ice cubes, coconut cream (reserve the liquid for another use), rum, simple syrup, lime leaves, and lime juice in a blender. Blend until smooth and frothy. Pour into cocktail glasses. Garnish each with a pineapple slice. Makes 2 mocktails.

TIP

Makrut Lime Leaves

Makrut lime leaves are edible lime leaves often used in Thai cooking. They are highly fragrant with a perfumed quality and an intense citrus flavor. They can be found in the produce section of many well-stocked grocery stores or in Asian markets.

MELON SLUSH

This is a great way to use up leftover bits of cantaloupe or honeydew that didn't get eaten at Sunday brunch. After work the next day, simply throw them into a blender with a little zero-proof vodka, simple syrup, lime juice, and ice cubes, and you have a revitalizing cocktail after a hard day. Melon season is June through August, so this one is a summer must.

GLASS: Coupe	GARNISH: Melon slice

¼ large ripe cantaloupe or honeydew, cut into cubes

1½ oz/45 ml fresh lime juice

1 oz/30 ml high-quality zero-proof vodka

1 oz/30 ml Simple Syrup (see Tip, page 20)

7 ice cubes

Melon slice, for garnish

Put the melon cubes in a blender with the lime juice, vodka, simple syrup, and ice cubes. Blend until slushy, adding water if needed. Transfer to a cocktail glass and garnish with a melon slice. Makes 1 mocktail.

NECTARINE BELLINI

When summer nectarines are getting a little overripe in the fruit bowl, turn them into a quick puree with a little simple syrup, then blend them with sparkling nonalcoholic white wine. Sipped out of a Champagne flute, it'll make you feel very fancy. The original Bellini was made with peach puree, so feel free to use peaches for this, too.

GLASS: Champagne flute	GARNISH: Nectarine slice

¾ oz/22 ml nectarine puree (see Tip, page 69)

1 oz/30 ml fresh lemon juice

Chilled high-quality nonalcoholic sparkling white wine

Nectarine slice, for garnish

Add the nectarine puree and lemon juice to a Champagne flute. Top with sparkling wine and stir gently. Garnish with a nectarine slice. Makes 1 mocktail.

Fruit Puree

In a blender, combine fruit, such as stemmed and seeded ripe Fuyu persimmons; peeled, pitted ripe nectarines or peaches; or peeled and pitted mango, with water or Simple Syrup (see Tip, page 20), using a little at a time depending on how sweet the fruit is, and puree until smooth.

PEACH-ROSEMARY TONIC

Rosemary's piney flavor has a strong affinity with stone fruit, so I used it as inspiration for this simple mocktail based on peach shrub. Remember, a little goes a long way with rosemary, so you don't want to use too much or it will overpower the drink.

GLASS: Highball or Collins	GARNISH: Peach slice and small rosemary sprig

A few fresh rosemary leaves

4 oz/120 ml peach shrub

Chilled tonic water

Peach slice, for garnish

Small rosemary sprig, for garnish

In a mixing glass, muddle the rosemary leaves. Add the peach shrub and ice and stir well. Strain into a cocktail glass filled with ice and top with chilled tonic water. Stir briefly. Garnish with a peach slice and a small rosemary sprig. Makes 1 mocktail.

NA STOUT FLOAT

On a hot summer night, a mocktail containing ice cream is a welcome treat. Guinness, arguably the most famous stout producer of all, now makes a zero-alcohol version of its flagship ale. It even comes in a can with the special gadget that makes the head foam up perfectly. It's the ideal choice for this recipe.

GLASS: Pint glass	GARNISH: Chocolate shavings

1 pint/450 g premium vanilla ice cream
Chocolate Syrup (see Tip, page 75) or store-bought
1 can (14.9 oz/420 ml) chilled nonalcoholic stout
Chocolate shavings, for garnish

Using an ice cream scoop, scoop 3 scoops of ice cream into each cocktail glass. Drizzle each generously with chocolate syrup. Open the can of stout and slowly pour it over the ice cream (you may not need all of it). Garnish with chocolate shavings. Makes 2 mocktails.

Chocolate Syrup

In a saucepan, whisk together 6 Tbsp/50 g unsweetened cocoa powder, ½ cup/100 g granulated sugar, and 4 oz/120 ml water. Set over medium heat and bring just to a simmer. Decrease the heat a simmer and cook, whisking, until thickened, about 3 minutes. Remove from the heat and stir in ½ tsp vanilla extract and a pinch of salt. Let cool completely. Makes 10 oz/300 ml.

SANSGRIA

This recipe is perfect for a three-day-weekend backyard barbecue. Inspired by Spanish sangria, I named it sansgria as a nod to the French word for "lacking." But you won't find it missing anything if you pick a high-quality nonalcoholic red wine and your favorite combination of fresh fruits.

GLASS: Wineglass	GARNISH: Sliced fruit and mint sprig
1 tart green apple, cored and diced	½ cup/75 g halved fresh strawberries
1 small grapefruit, thinly sliced, then cut into eighths	2 bottles (750 ml) high-quality nonalcoholic red wine
1 orange, thinly sliced, then cut into eighths	2 oz/60 ml high-quality zero-proof orange liqueur
1 lemon, quartered length-wise, then cut into quarters	2 oz/60 ml high-quality zero-proof vodka
½ cup/75 g fresh raspberries	Fresh mint sprig, for garnish

Put the apple, citrus fruits, and berries in a large pitcher. Pour in the wine, orange liqueur, and vodka and stir well. Chill overnight. Pour over ice to serve (the fruit becomes the garnish) and add a mint sprig. Makes 8–12 mocktails.

CUCUMBER GIMLETTE

For this recipe, I was inspired by the gimlet, a simple, three-ingredient cocktail. Thinking of a summer garden, I added cucumber as a fourth component. Gin and cucumbers are natural partners, their flavors complementing each other in numerous cocktail recipes. Tasting it, it's a match made in heaven.

GLASS: Martini or coupe	GARNISH: Cucumber slice

2-inch/5-cm piece English cucumber, peeled and diced

2 oz/60 ml high-quality zero-proof gin

1 oz/30 ml fresh lime juice

¾ oz/22 ml Simple Syrup (see Tip, page 20)

Cucumber slice, for garnish

In a cocktail shaker, muddle the diced cucumber. Add the gin, lime juice, and simple syrup. Add ice and shake until chilled. Strain into a cocktail glass and garnish with the cucumber slice. Makes 1 mocktail.

FALL

SPICED HIBISCUS AGUA FRESCA

I tried the flor de Jamaica special agua fresca at my local taqueria one day. Made from dried hibiscus flowers, it had a deep red color and herbaceous flavor. It inspired this recipe, spiced with cinnamon, sweetened with agave, and spiked with lemon juice for balance.

GLASS: Highball or Collins	GARNISH: Mint sprig
28 oz/840 ml water ⅓ cup/13 g dried hibiscus flowers 1 cinnamon stick	1 oz/30 ml agave nectar, or to taste Fresh lemon juice Fresh mint sprig, for garnish

In a small saucepan, bring the water to a boil. Remove from the heat and add the hibiscus flowers and cinnamon stick. Cover and let the mixture stand for 10 minutes. Strain the mixture into a pitcher. Add the agave nectar and stir well. Refrigerate until very cold.

To serve, taste the mixture and add more agave and lemon juice to taste. Pour into glasses and garnish with mint. Makes 4 mocktails.

PEARTINI

|

Unlike their boozy counterparts, zero-proof liquors typically are not great for sipping straight. So when it came to considering drinks like mock martinis, I found the best way to show off zero-proof vodka was to incorporate seasonal fruit, as I did here with autumn pears. The floral elderflower syrup is a sophisticated accent.

GLASS: Martini or coupe	GARNISH: Lime slice

½ large very ripe pear

2 oz/60 ml high-quality zero-proof vodka

½ oz/15 ml fresh lime juice

½ oz/15 ml elderflower syrup

Pinch of kosher salt

Lime slice, for garnish

Peel, core, and dice the pear, then place it in a cocktail shaker. Muddle it well. Add the vodka, lime juice, elderflower syrup, and salt. Add ice and shake until chilled. Strain into a cocktail glass and garnish with a lime twist. Makes 1 mocktail.

MICHELLE-ADA

My version of a Michelada blends tomato juice with Mexican-style spices, Worcestershire sauce, hot sauce, and beer. Have fun experimenting with different types of NA beer; I like a hoppy IPA, but traditionally in Mexico they would use a lager.

GLASS: Highball	GARNISH: Lime wedges
12 oz/360 ml chilled fresh tomato juice	6 dashes Worcestershire sauce, or to taste
12 oz/360 ml chilled nonalcoholic beer	Hot sauce, to taste
2 oz/60 ml fresh lime juice	Chile Salt (see Tip, page 89)
2 tsp chili powder	Lime wedges, for garnish

In a pitcher, combine the tomato juice, beer, lime juice, chili powder, Worcestershire sauce, and hot saucee. Stir to blend.

To prepare the glasses, sprinkle the chile salt onto a small plate. Wipe a lime wedge around the rims of the cocktail glasses, then dip the rims into the salt mixture. Fill the glasses with ice, then divide the tomato mixture among the glasses. Garnish with lime wedges. Makes 2–4 mocktails.

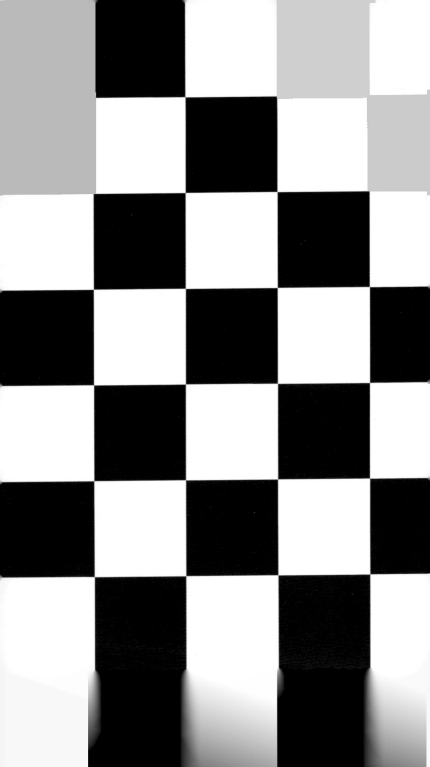

Chile Salt

Mix together 1 Tbsp kosher salt,
1 Tbsp smoked paprika,
and 1 Tbsp ancho chile powder.

NOGRONI

One week every September is designated
"Negroni" week in the United States, so I wanted
to develop a mocktail appropriate for lovers of the
dark red, pleasantly astringent, gin-based cocktail.
Nonalcoholic bitters come in different flavors;
orange bitters would be delicious here as well.

GLASS: Lowball	GARNISH: Orange slice

2 oz/60 ml high-quality zero-proof gin

½ oz/15 ml nonalcoholic red vermouth

½ oz/15 ml high-quality nonalcoholic Italian-style aperitif

¼ oz/7 ml Juniper Simple Syrup (see Tip, page 20)

4–5 dashes nonalcoholic bitters

Orange twist, for garnish

In a cocktail shaker, add the gin, vermouth, aperitif, simple
syrup, and bitters. Add ice and shake until chilled. Strain into
a cocktail glass filled with ice and garnish with an orange
twist. Makes 1 mocktail.

FRENCHIE 75

Dating from World War I, the French 75 cocktail was an elegant gin-and-Champagne sip served in sophisticated bars. Using a zero-proof craft gin and high-quality sparkling wine, it's easy to create a mocktail version any night of the week.

GLASS: Champagne flute or coupe	GARNISH: Lemon twist

1 oz/30 ml high-quality zero-proof gin

1 oz/30 ml Juniper Simple Syrup (see Tip, page 20)

½ oz/15 ml fresh lemon juice

5 oz/150 ml well-chilled high-quality nonalcoholic sparkling white wine

Lemon twist, for garnish

In a cocktail glass, add the gin, simple syrup, and lemon juice, then top with the sparkling wine. Garnish with a lemon twist. Makes 1 mocktail.

Making Citrus Twists

There are special tools for making lemon, lime, or orange twists, but they're often not sharp enough to work with easily. A paring knife does the job every time. Use a sharp one to cut a long, thin strip from the center of the fruit, aiming to remove just the colored part of the skin. Lay the strip on a cutting board and clean up any white pith if needed. If you like, wind the strip around your finger or a chopstick to shape it into a pretty spiral.

ESPRESSO-TINI

I always thought the traditional espresso martini was oxymoronic: the dulling power of the vodka canceling out the stimulating effect of the espresso. In this mocktail, the choice is yours—rousing or relaxing, depending on whether you opt for regular or decaf espresso, as there are no canceling effects from alcohol. The addition of half-and-half will help give the drink a light froth on top.

GLASS: Martini	GARNISH: Whole coffee beans

1½ oz/45 ml high-quality zero-proof coffee liqueur
1½ oz/45 ml high-quality zero-proof vodka
1 oz/30 ml freshly brewed espresso, cooled
½ oz/15 ml Vanilla Simple Syrup (see Tip, page 21)
Splash of half-and-half or full-fat oat milk (optional)
Whole coffee beans, for garnish

In a cocktail shaker, add the coffee liqueur, vodka, espresso, simple syrup, and half-and-half (if using). Add ice and shake until chilled. Strain into a cocktail glass and garnish with coffee beans. Makes 1 mocktail.

SPICY CRANRITA

Here is a bright, spicy update on a classic margarita featuring cranberry juice and fresh jalapeños. To tame the spiciness, remove the seeds from the jalapeño.

GLASS: Lowball	GARNISH: Sliced jalapeños
2 tsp salt, for the rim 1 tsp sugar, for the rim Lime wedge, for the rim 1½ oz/45 ml unsweetened cranberry juice 1½ oz/45 ml high-quality zero-proof tequila	½ small jalapeño chile, thinly sliced, plus more for garnish 1 oz/30 ml fresh lime juice ¾–1 oz/22–30 ml pure maple syrup

To prepare the glass, sprinkle the salt and sugar onto a small plate. Wipe the lime wedge around the rim of the cocktail glass, then dip the rim into the salt and sugar mixture. Fill the glass with ice.

In a cocktail shaker, add the cranberry juice, tequila, jalapeño slices, lime juice, and maple syrup. Add ice and shake until chilled. Strain into the prepared cocktail glass and garnish with more jalapeño slices. Makes 1 mocktail.

POMEGRANATE COSMO

Pomegranate juice, which is high in antioxidants and polyphenols, has known health benefits. But I bet you won't care when you shake it with zero-proof vodka, orange liqueur, and just-squeezed lime juice and serve it in a martini glass, Sex and the City style.

GLASS: Martini or coupe	GARNISH: Pomegranate arils

3 oz/90 ml high-quality zero-proof vodka

2 oz/60 ml unsweetened pomegranate juice

1 oz/30 ml fresh lime juice

1 oz/30 ml high-quality zero-proof orange liqueur

Pomegranate arils, for garnish

In a cocktail shaker, add the vodka, pomegranate juice, lime juice, and orange liqueur. Add ice and shake until chilled. Strain into a cocktail glass and garnish with the pomegranate arils. Makes 1 mocktail.

COFFEE CLATCH

When the weather starts to turn cold, I like to be a bit more indulgent with my mocktails. This mocktail, based on a white Russian, is a good choice when you want something sweet, creamy, and comforting. If you're opting for the oat milk, be sure to look for the full-fat variety (Oatly has one) to achieve the right consistency.

GLASS: Old fashioned or highball	GARNISH: Espresso powder

1½ oz/45 ml high-quality zero-proof coffee liqueur

1½ oz/45 ml high-quality zero-proof vodka

1 oz/30 ml Brown Sugar Simple Syrup (see Tip, page 20)

6 oz/180 ml cold half-and-half or full-fat oat milk

Espresso powder, for garnish

Fill a cocktail glass with ice cubes. Pour in the coffee liqueur, vodka, and simple syrup and stir gently. Slowly pour in the half-and-half over the back of a spoon to create a layered effect. Garnish with espresso powder. Makes 1 mocktail.

PUMPKIN SPICE TODDY

It wouldn't be fall without pumpkin spice, so I created a recipe that can help you satisfy that flavor urge at home, anytime you like. This recipe is also a good way to use up the pie spices that you buy only once a year and never know what to do with. My advice: Make multiples; this recipe is a crowd-pleaser.

GLASS: Mug	GARNISH: Cinnamon stick
1 Tbsp pumpkin puree (not pumpkin pie filling)	½ oz/15 ml fresh lemon juice
¼ tsp ground cinnamon	½ oz/15 ml pure maple syrup
⅛ tsp ground ginger	5 oz/150 ml boiling water
⅛ tsp ground allspice	Cinnamon stick, for garnish
Pinch of ground cloves	Lemon wheel, for garnish
2 oz/60 ml high-quality zero-proof whiskey or bourbon	

In a preheated coffee mug, mix together the pumpkin puree, cinnamon, ginger, allspice, and cloves. Add the whiskey, lemon juice, and maple syrup and stir well. Stir in the boiling water. Garnish with a cinnamon stick and lemon wheel, and serve warm. Makes 1 mocktail.

SOUR PERSIMMON

Fuyu persimmons are a quintessential fall fruit with a cult following here in Northern California. This time of year, they are overflowing at farmers' markets. Pureed, they make a unique addition to a zero-proof take on a classic sour cocktail. If you use a Hachiya persimmon, decrease the amount of simple syrup when you make the puree.

GLASS: Coupe	GARNISH: Dried Persimmon slice

2 oz/60 ml high-quality zero-proof gin

1½ oz/45 ml Fuyu persimmon puree (see Tip, page 69)

1 oz/30 ml fresh grapefruit juice

½ oz/15 ml fresh lime juice

Dried persimmon slice, for garnish

In a cocktail shaker, add the gin, persimmon puree, grapefruit juice, and lime juice. Add ice and shake until chilled. Strain into a cocktail glass and garnish with a dried persimmon slice. Makes 1 mocktail.

CRANBERRY ROYALE

Here, cranberry juice and black currant syrup gild a NA version of a French kir royale. As with any cocktail based on sparkling wine, you'll want to be sure you choose a nonalcoholic sparkler that tastes delicious on its own. I encourage you to experiment to find your favorites.

GLASS: Champagne flute	GARNISH: Sugar rim and fresh cranberry
Sugar, for the rim Lemon wedge, for the rim 4 oz/120 ml chilled unsweetened cranberry juice ½ oz/15 ml fresh lemon juice	½ oz/15 ml black currant syrup High-quality nonalcoholic sparkling white wine Fresh cranberry, for garnish

To prepare the Champagne flute, sprinkle sugar onto a small plate. Wipe the lemon wedge around the rim of the flute, then dip the rim into the sugar.

To the prepared glass, add the cranberry juice, and lemon juice, black currant syrup and top with the sparkling wine. Garnish with a fresh cranberry. Makes 1 mocktail.

LIQUID APPLE PIE

On a cold evening, warm up with a nonalcoholic take on mulled cider fortified with zero-proof rum. To make prep easier, put the small spices in a tea ball for infusing. This recipe also works well with zero-proof whiskey or bourbon. Pro tip: This also makes a great brunch drink and is easy to multiply for a crowd.

GLASS: Mug	GARNISH: Apple slice

10 oz/300 ml unfiltered apple cider

4 allspice berries

2 whole cloves

1 cinnamon stick

3 oz/90 ml high-quality zero-proof rum

Apple slices, for garnish

In a small saucepan, combine the cider, allspice, cloves, and cinnamon stick and warm over medium-high heat until the mixture comes to a simmer. Remove from the heat, cover, and let steep for 5 minutes. Add 1½ oz/45 ml rum to each mug. Divide the warm cider mixture between the mugs and serve warm, garnished with apple slices. Makes 2 mocktails.

WINTER

TURMERIC LEMON POP

Turmeric has powerful anti-inflammatory properties, which make it a good choice to drink during winter cold season. It is a gorgeous deep-yellow color, which adds to the stunning appearance of this mocktail.

GLASS: Martini	GARNISH: Lemon wheel
Sugar, for the rim	1½ oz/45 ml fresh lemon juice
Finely grated lemon zest, for the rim	1 oz/30 ml Turmeric Simple Syrup (see Tip, page 21)
Lemon wedge, for the rim	Lemon twist, for garnish
2 oz/60 ml high-quality zero-proof vodka	

To prepare the cocktail glass, sprinkle sugar and lemon zest onto a small plate. Rub together with your fingers until the mixture is tinted yellow and fragrant. Wipe the lemon wedge around the rim of a martini glass, then dip the rim into the sugar mixture.

In a cocktail shaker, add the vodka, lemon juice, and simple syrup. Add ice and shake until chilled. Strain into a cocktail glass and garnish with a lemon wheel. Makes 1 mocktail.

DANDY ALEXANDER

For my take on a brandy Alexander, I use zero-proof whiskey, which has the smoky, woody notes that the original brandy offers. With the addition of chocolate syrup, brown sugar syrup, cream, and a nutmeg garnish, this recipe gets really close to the original.

GLASS: Coupe or martini	GARNISH: Grated nutmeg

2 oz/60 ml high-quality zero-proof whiskey

1 oz/30 ml Chocolate Syrup (see Tip, page 75) or store-bought

1 oz/30 ml Brown Sugar Simple Syrup (see Tip, page 20)

1 oz/30 ml heavy cream

Grated nutmeg, for garnish

In a cocktail shaker, add the whiskey, chocolate syrup, simple syrup, and cream. Add ice and shake until chilled. Pour into a cocktail glass. Garnish with grated nutmeg. Makes 1 mocktail.

THE JINERVA

Years ago, I found myself spontaneously entertaining extended family and came up with an original cocktail with what I had on hand in the kitchen. It turned out to be a hit. My husband dubbed it "The Jinerva," which was a play on both the gin I used and my name, Jennifer. Here is the mocktail version, which made it to book form first.

GLASS: Old fashioned or lowball	GARNISH: Lime wedge

1 oz/30 ml dark agave nectar

1 oz/30 ml fresh lime juice

2 oz/60 ml high-quality zero-proof gin

Sparkling water

Lime wedge, for garnish

In a cocktail glass, combine the agave nectar and lime juice and stir well. Add the gin and fill with ice. Top with sparkling water and garnish with a lime wedge. Makes 1 mocktail.

IRISH-ISH COFFEE

One of the first places my mom took me when we visited San Francisco was the Buena Vista, a world-famous Irish coffee spot near Fisherman's Wharf. Even though I was only seventeen at the time, I guess I looked the part—the bartender didn't blink when my mom ordered an Irish coffee for each of us. This is my ode to that trip, with a couple of modern upgrades.

GLASS: Mug	GARNISH: Espresso powder and cinnamon sticks

2 demerara sugar cubes

6 oz/180 ml strong, hot, dark-roast brewed coffee

2 oz/60 ml high-quality zero-proof whiskey

Coconut Whipped Cream (see Tip, page 123)

Espresso powder and cinnamon sticks, for garnish

Put the sugar cubes in a preheated mug and fill with coffee. Stir until the sugar is dissolved. Add the whiskey and stir briefly. Top with a generous amount of coconut whipped cream, garnish with espresso powder and cinnamon sticks, and serve warm. Makes 1 mocktail.

Coconut Whipped Cream

Chill one can (14 oz/390 ml) of full-fat coconut milk for 24 hours. Using a chilled bowl and whisk attachment on a stand mixer, beat the solid cap of cream on top of the coconut milk (reserve the liquid for another use) with 2 Tbsp powdered sugar and 1 tsp pure vanilla extract until light and fluffy.

PINK PALOMITA

The authentic Mexican paloma is simply tequila and grapefruit soda. But here, I take advantage of the winter citrus fruit that is so delicious this time of year and blend it into a refreshing inauthentic paloma with zero-proof spirits and maple syrup for a little smoky sweetness.

GLASS: Old fashioned or lowball	GARNISH: Pink grapefruit slice

2 oz/60 ml high-quality zero-proof tequila

2 oz/60 ml fresh pink grapefruit juice

½ oz/15 ml fresh lime juice

¼ oz/7 ml maple syrup

Pinch of salt

Pink grapefruit slice, for garnish

In a cocktail shaker, add the tequila, grapefruit juice, lime juice, maple syrup, and salt. Add ice and shake until chilled. Strain into a cocktail glass filled with ice and garnish with a grapefruit slice. Makes 1 mocktail.

ROSEMARY MULE

*For this take on a traditional Moscow mule,
I use rosemary-infused simple syrup, which goes
surprisingly well with the spicy flavors of the ginger
beer. Take care when buying ginger beer—most
are nonalcoholic (less than 0.5% alcohol by volume),
but a few brands out there bump up the ABV.*

GLASS: Copper mule mug	GARNISH: Rosemary sprig and lime wedge

3 oz/90 ml ginger beer

2 oz/60 ml high-quality zero-proof vodka

½ oz/15 ml fresh lemon juice

½ oz/15 ml Rosemary Simple Syrup (see Tip, page 21)

Rosemary sprig, for garnish

Lime wedge, for garnish

In a mixing glass, add the ginger beer, vodka, lemon juice, and simple syrup. Add ice and stir until chilled. Strain into a copper mug filled with crushed ice and garnish with a rosemary sprig and lime wedge. Makes 1 mocktail.

CINNAMON HOT TODDY

*Long considered a remedy for a cold, a hot toddy
is a must-have in your repertoire during the winter
months. This zero-proof version starts with
steeped cinnamon tea for a spicy change of pace.
I'm an advocate of consuming local honey, which is
supposedly helpful for fighting local toxins
and helping support immunity.*

GLASS: Mug	GARNISH: Cinnamon stick
4 oz/120 ml hot water	½ oz/15 ml fresh lemon juice
1 cinnamon tea bag	½ oz/15 ml local honey
2 oz/60 ml zero-proof whiskey	Cinnamon stick, for garnish

In a preheated mug, pour the hot water over the tea bag,
cover to keep warm, and let it steep for 5 minutes. Discard
the tea bag. Add the whiskey, lemon juice, and honey and stir
well. Garnish with pomegranate arils and a cinnamon stick
and serve warm. Makes 1 mocktail.

PARTY PUNCH

|

Winter holiday season provides many opportunities to celebrate with friends and family, and one of my favorite retro offerings is to set out a punch bowl on the buffet for self-serve drinks.

GLASS: Old fashioned or lowball	GARNISH: Pomegranate arils and rosemary sprigs
1 Granny Smith apple, peeled, cored, and diced small	2 oz/60 ml fresh lemon juice
1 Honeycrisp apple, peeled, cored, and diced small	Ice Ring (see Tip, page 133)
32 oz/960 ml apple cider	1 bottle (750 ml) chilled high-quality nonalcoholic sparkling white wine
12 oz/360 ml high-quality zero-proof whiskey	Pomegranate arils and rosemary sprigs, for garnish

Place the apples, apple cider, whiskey, and lemon juice in a pitcher and chill until very cold.

When ready to serve, put the ice ring in a punch bowl and pour the mixture into the bowl. Pour in the sparkling wine. Ladle the punch into small glasses filled with ice. Garnish with pomegranate arils and rosemary sprigs. Makes 10 mocktails.

TIP

Ice Ring

Layer fresh cranberries, pomegranate arils, and rosemary sprigs in a Bundt pan and fill with water, juice, or nonalcoholic wine. Freeze overnight. To unmold, dip the pan in hot water until the ice starts to loosen around the edges. Invert onto a plate. Pop into the punch bowl before adding the punch ingredients.

EGGNOGGIN

Trust me, your family will thank you for making this recipe. It is a huge upgrade from store-bought eggnog. The key to its special flavor is to use a whole nutmeg and grate it fresh using a Microplane. Don't try to substitute preground nutmeg—it just won't taste right. This is a very sweet drink. Just go with it—it's holiday season.

GLASS: Coupe	GARNISH: Freshly grated nutmeg and star anise
Eggnog Base (see Tip, page 137)	Freshly grated nutmeg, for garnish
8 oz/240 ml high-quality zero-proof whiskey, bourbon, or dark rum	4 star anise for garnish (optional)

Remove the eggnog base from the refrigerator and stir in the whiskey, bourbon, or rum. Divide among cocktail glasses and garnish with grated nutmeg and star anise (if using). Makes 4 mocktails.

Eggnog Base

In a large heatproof bowl, whisk 4 large egg yolks and ¾ cup/150g sugar until creamy and lemon colored, 1–2 minutes. In a saucepan over medium heat, warm 12 oz/360 ml whole milk, 6 oz/180 ml heavy cream, 1 tsp freshly grated nutmeg, ½ tsp ground cinnamon, ½ tsp freshly ground pepper, and ⅛ tsp kosher salt until just starting to bubble around the edges. Remove from the heat. While whisking the yolk mixture, slowly ladle in about 2 oz/60 ml of the hot milk mixture. Continue to whisk in the hot milk mixture 2 oz/60 ml at a time until half of it is added, then add the milk-yolk mixture to the saucepan. Place over medium heat and bring the mixture just to a simmer, stirring constantly. Remove from the heat. Pour the mixture into a bowl set over an ice bath to cool down quickly. When the mixture is cool, transfer it to the refrigerator to cool completely, preferably overnight.

BLOOD ORANGE SPARKLER

Every December, I wait for blood oranges to come to the farmers' markets. Their deep-red color and sweet, slightly bitter flavor are worth waiting for. In this variation of a mimosa, you can play with the ratio of juice to wine to suit your taste. And feel free to use other citrus juices, like grapefruit, tangerine, orange, or a combination.

GLASS: Wineglass or Champagne flute	GARNISH: Blood orange slice

4 oz/120 ml chilled fresh blood orange juice

½ oz/15 ml high-quality zero-proof orange liqueur (optional)

Chilled high-quality nonalcoholic sparkling wine

Blood orange slice, for garnish

Pour the juice into a cocktail glass. Add the liqueur (if using) and top with the sparkling wine. Garnish with a blood orange slice. Makes 1 mocktail.

WINTER SPICED MULLED WINE

This warm, spiced wine concoction is perfect for a last-minute get-together with colleagues on a cold winter evening.

GLASS: Mug	GARNISH: Cinnamon stick, star anise, and orange slices
1 bottle (750 ml) high-quality nonalcoholic red wine	3 cinnamon sticks, broken in half
8 oz/240 ml unfiltered apple cider	6 whole cloves
½ cup/100 g sugar	Zest of 1 lemon, removed in strips
1 orange, sliced ¼ inch/6 mm thick	½ bay leaf (optional)
	Cinnamon stick, star anise, and orange slices, for garnish

In a heavy saucepan, combine the wine, cider, sugar, orange slices, cinnamon sticks, cloves, lemon zest, and bay leaf (if using). Warm slowly over low heat for at least 1 hour.

Remove the bay leaf. Ladle into mugs to serve, garnished with a cinnamon stick, star anise, and orange slices. Makes 6 mocktails.

GIN FIZZY

Here is my take on the classic gin fizz, egg white and all. The secret to success here is to first shake the ingredients without ice to give the egg white time to develop the desired silky texture. Then, add ice and shake until the drink is chilled.

GLASS: Highball or Collins	GARNISH: Lemon slice
2 oz/60 ml high-quality zero-proof gin 1 oz/30 ml fresh lemon juice ¾ oz/22 ml Juniper Simple Syrup (see Tip, page 20)	1 large fresh egg white* Chilled sparkling water Lemon slice, for garnish

Add the gin, lemon juice, simple syrup, and egg white to a cocktail shaker and shake for about 15 seconds. Add ice to the cocktail shaker and shake vigorously until the egg white is frothy and the mixture is chilled. Strain into a cocktail glass filled halfway with ice. Top with sparkling water and garnish with a lemon slice. Makes 1 mocktail.

* If you have health and safety concerns, you may wish to avoid mocktails or cocktails made with raw egg whites.

NA SPARKLING WINE COCKTAIL

Based on the classic Champagne cocktail, this is the perfect choice for a New Year's Eve toast—it's elegant and festive and the best way to start off a Dry January. Due to the surging popularity of low- or no-ABV drinks, there are many nonalcoholic sparkling wines available these days. The bubbles make me feel like I'm drinking something special.

GLASS: Champagne flute	GARNISH: Lemon twist

1 sugar cube

Nonalcoholic bitters

½ oz/15 ml high-quality zero-proof white vermouth

High-quality nonalcoholic sparkling white wine

Lemon twist, for garnish

Put the sugar cube in a Champagne flute and add bitters until completely soaked. Pour in the vermouth. Add the sparkling wine until the glass is full. Garnish with a lemon twist. Makes 1 mocktail.

RESOURCES

Here are some resources that are useful for finding the ingredients called for in this book and stocking your home mocktail bar.

Boisson

All you need to stock a home bar, from NA wines, beers, and spirits to mixers and accessories. There are brick-and-mortar retail stores in New York City, Los Angeles, and San Francisco (and expanding), but they will ship anywhere legally allowed via their website. boisson.co

Happy Girl Kitchen

Look to them for shrubs, drink garnishes, and the best-ever dry-farmed tomato juice. happygirlkitchen.com

Proxies

Rather than de-alcoholized wine, proxies
are blends of wine grapes, teas, spices,
and other fruits that are designed by
sommeliers and chefs to match the
weight, acidity, tannins, and food pairing
capability—everything we love about
wine—without the alcohol. They're my
favorite type of NA wine I've tasted so
far. drinkproxies.com

Total Wine and More

A national chain store that offers an
expanding selection of NA products,
depending on location. They have some
shipping capacity, but it is location
specific. totalwine.com

INDEX

Index